Eyes of Soul

Biju Ramachandran

BookLeaf Publishing

India | USA | UK

Presentation by *BookLeaf Publishing*

Web: www.bookleafpub.com

E-mail: info@bookleafpub.com

ISBN: 9789360943202

First edition 2024

ACKNOWLEDGEMENT

I wish to express my heartfelt gratitude to my beloved mother, sister, wife, and son for their unwavering support and endless encouragement.

PREFACE

Within these pages, you will find a humble offering—a heartfelt tribute to the boundless admiration the author holds for the intricate mosaic of our Indian culture and the profound wellspring of wisdom that flows from its philosophical heritage.

This endeavour is, at its core, a sincere attempt to convey the splendour and depth of these cherished facets, presented with utmost humility and a heartfelt aspiration to kindle contemplation and appreciation in the hearts of those who journey through these verses.

Manikarnika Ghat

After Ganga Aarti, I wandered to Manikarnika,
followed the steps down to the burning ghat
and reached where logs lay piled up,
ready for corpses, fire and funerals!

Processions from galis poured with chants
"Ram naam satya hai' and fed bodies
all day and night! Doesn't this ever stop?
Hungry ghats and the cycle of birth and death!

Several funeral pyres and flames blazed;
Dragons danced and breathed fireflies and Oms!
Bells, cymbals, and drums matched fever-pitch
chants!
There stood stunned pilgrims drunk in a divine
trance!

Fire tongues licked the body and then
swallowed.
Shiva slowly untangled knots and released souls.
Imagine souls rising to open heaven's door so
close!
Or is this Moksha, the break of the rebirth cycle?

Tired goats and dogs rested on dirty ghat steps,
with cows, bulls and buffaloes of Varanasi.
Birds and monkeys are perched somewhere
on that mesmerising mystical night at Ghats!

The soft night is slowly growing around,
and little stars are sprouting from eternity.
Moon is ready to rise and shine in the east.
Lover wind danced and swept ghats cold!

Born pure at Gangotri, the divine stream has
turned dark, bearing the waste and sins of
generations!
With the patience of an ultimate mother,
Ganga Ma blesses her trampling children!

I, too, am guilty, and I beg for forgiveness!
Ganga, Ghat, Agni, Akash aur Vayu- Neti, Neti!
I lay at your feet, ready to redeem Ma!
Vande Mataram! My land! My home!

I sat on the roots and wept!

I went back to my dream home,
A home in nature where I started...
Day after day, my parents built
that home, now frozen in the past!

I looked at the tree for my old nest,
Now fallen, dead, with broken homes...
Everything looked so different!
I sat on the roots and wept!

I searched for friends but found none,
Then, I saw a family, not the one I knew,
Not my old friends from before!
I sat on the roots and wept!

I wanted to go back to the fun,
But found a graveyard of memories,
Broken homes and lost friendships.
I sat on the roots and wept!

This was my place; was it still?
Do I still belong here?
Why did I ever leave and fly away?
I sat on the roots and wept!

Then, a soft voice from the last root,
"Look inside for God." Who?
The one I forgot while living?
I sat on the roots and wept!

I looked deep inside and saw my young self,
I reached out and made friends again...
Will I find peace? I'm not sure yet.
I sat on the roots and wept!

Lady paddy reapers of Kerala

I was just a boy when I saw this scene,
Still vivid, like a movie in my memory.

Golden grains bending on straw,
Ripe and ready in Kerala's fields.

Peasant women in worn lungis and shirts,
Heads covered with areca nut caps.

Betel nut paan moving in their humming
mouths,
Sickles in hand, they were ready for work.

The wet sickles glinted in the sun,
Strong arms moving in a steady rhythm.

Songs from unknown poets
Rose and fell with the warm wind.

Knee-deep in water, sweat dripped down,
Forming little streams.

The wind cooled them, soaked their clothes,
Carrying the scents of fresh-cut paddy and earth.

Morning's work done, they walked in line,
Across the narrow field paths.

Carrying bundles of paddy on their heads,
Under the watchful eyes of birds, sun, and clear
sky.

Spicy buttermilk to quench their thirst,
Rationed rice and fish curry for a modest meal.

Their lunch packed in thin banana leaves,
While we waited, tired kids and cows, in the
grass.

Alone in the library

I drove to the library,
Last week of December,
A chilly, dark grey day,
A Saturday afternoon.

Alone on the top floor,
In Canterbury's university library.
A sign said, "Shhh!!!"
"Work alone, in silence."

I started writing,
Time slipped away unnoticed.
I heard someone talking,
But no one was around.

I walked, no one in sight.

Paused, looked out the glass wall.
There stood Canterbury Cathedral's shadow,
Through a misty screen.

Heard more voices, saw no one,
They said, "Please read me,"
"No, pick me, it's been ten years!"
"Me first, it's been 15, please!"

A strong voice demanded,
"I'm in a library, not a charity shop,
I was a leader; respect me!
Read me now, or release me!"

Internet, media, social media,
You don't read us anymore!
Kindles, audiobooks, podcasts,
You don't need us anymore!

"Is this a museum? Are we trapped?"
"You can't lock up our ideas,"
"They'll break free, find the right minds."
"Burn down this library," yelled a rebel voice.

"Are you a writer here alone,
On a holiday morning?
Do something worth writing,
Or write something worth reading!"
The diplomat's voice rose, and chaos ensued.

Lights flickered, I grabbed my bag, ran
Down three floors in a flash,
Out into a deep breath of cold air,
The wind hugged and comforted me.

A few steps away, I looked back,
The library stood alone in the dark.
The front glass door read, "Library closed,
During Christmas and New Year."

Stop the war!

A mother's love is cold!
She's crying alone in the dark,
Her tears burn on her aged cheek.
Can the earth bear this pain?

A mother's curse is deep and hard!
Too lofty for any leader or ruler!
If she speaks it out loud,
Can anyone bear its weight?

Her husband was lost in war,
Their home is now ruined.
All their love and memories are gone!
How can a Mother face this?

Now, her son returned,
But only as a silent, lifeless form.
It is in a box, so small, so cold!
Who can stand to see this?

Centuries echoed the wail
that shattered mothers gave!
Its wave rose sky-high, and
empires trembled and crumbled!

This is a lesson from history:
The spirit of a suffering mother
It will crush the mightiest power.
Stop the war, please! STOP THE WAR!!

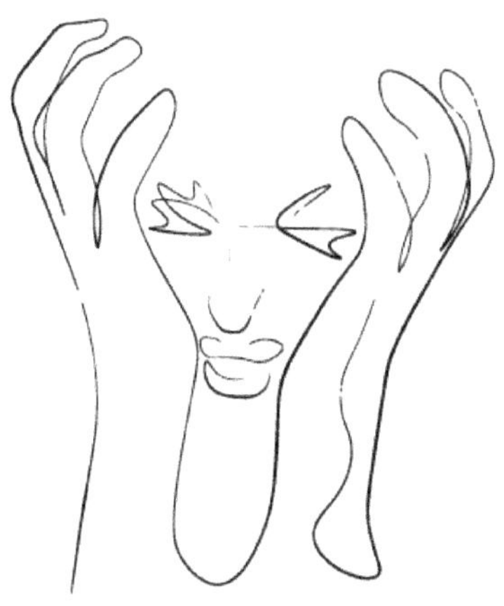

Wake up!

In my dream, it rains,
Held in bed's gentle shackles.
Warm in a blanket's embrace,
Cold's subtle, creeping claws.

Half-open, the window sways,
Eyes closed, yet ears alert.
Dead leaves hum a rustle-tune,
Chorus birds sing in the background.

Drumbeats stir the moist air,
Soft, light strokes with tender care.
"Why wake me from my slumber?
Let me dwell in my dreams, please!"

"Worn with sorrows unbearable,
Heart tired, dreams shattered!
Don't wake my sleeping eyes,
In dreams, my solace lies."

"Stop the rain drum; delay the day,
In this dream, I wish to stay.
Let sleep return; dreams replay,
Music paused, drummer away!"

But the stage is set, lights ablaze!
Music on! "Wake up, my girl! Rock the Day!"
Rings dead Nana's voice, long gone, yet near!
Inspiring life, clearing melancholy!

Eyes open, Chrysalis gently stirs,
stretches soft wings, and the shell cracks!
In that wakeful moment, unique...
Life's path unfolds; Buddha smiles!

In Search of Me

Action, Actions, More Actions!
Pause! Reflect! Meditate!!
"An unexamined life..."
Is this my story, my history?

Past, present, future,
They're all stitched together.
Teach me to understand,
Link past to future, show me how to create.

People, events, missing pieces...
I can't find myself in it all!
I've searched deep inside,
But it feels like there's nothing left.

Who am I? What's my purpose? Where do I fit?
I can't find myself. Why am I here?
Is anyone out there? Does someone need me?

Eastern sages, Western thinkers, I need answers!

Please tell me soon, or I'll be lost,
Blown away like forgotten dust.
"Why should anyone remember?" you ask.
I don't know, but... oh, how I wish I did!

A Braveheart

I met a girl with a smile, despite her burns,
Her face, neck scarred, one arm gone.
She lost so much as a child, just like I felt lost.
We talked; I felt sorry, but for myself!

She's full of Hope, Dreams, and Plans.
Wants to be a Professor, studying to teach.
She writes with her foot, so gracefully!
This brave girl, she'll reach her dreams.

Here I am, restless and tired, lucky,
yet unfulfilled, helping at a medical camp.
I can't heal her wounds.
God, is she here to heal my soul?

She spoke with confidence, laughed, and joked.
I was moved, found something deep inside.
Felt grateful, wanted to touch her feet!
Indeed, God lives in this brave girl's heart.

Sea Goddess

I grew up by the sea,
Always watching its waves.
I loved the sea more each day,
Fascinated by its mystery.

In school, I learned about the sea,
Read tales of a sea goddess in books.
I dreamed of her underwater palace,
Hoping to visit one day!

As a young kid, swimming near the shore,
I felt a pull dragging me down.
Is it my big dream fish?
Or is it the sea goddess calling me?

The pull spun me around,

Like a fast merry-go-round.
I held tight to the merry-go-round.
Too fast it was! Merry no more!

I was a frightened child!
I thought of my parents,
prayed to the sea goddess,
And then, finally, I let go!

Suddenly, I saw a coral palace,
Mermaids and odd fishes all around.
They brought me to the palace,
Where the sea goddess sat on her throne.

The spinning stopped,
I wasn't moving anymore.
Was I thrown out? Spat out?
I can't recall even now!

Then someone shook me,
Voices around, my cough woke me!
Heard seagulls, felt the wind, the sun!
I was lying on the sandy shore!

Eyes closed, the sun too bright,
I opened them to see worried faces.
"Lucky boy, thank the sea goddess!"
Said an old man, walking away.

Death of an Indian Soldier

In obscurity, an Indian soldier fell,
Not in battle, nor by the enemy's shell.
In the barracks' quiet, his heart ceased to swell,
Shattered by life's cruel, unyielding spell.

Tall and robust, a figure of might,
His skin like night, his presence a sight.
Muscles bound tight, ready for the fight,
Yet fated never to prove his might.

To the world, he was but a wisp, unseen,
His heart, a vessel for love, so keen.
His breath drew deep, in love's hues serene,
A soul too vast, in a world too lean.

From toddler's laughter to the elder's sigh,
In his coastal village under the sky,
Admired by all, none could deny,
His departure at eighteen, a village's cry.

With each return, the village's pride,
A month of joy, with him by their side.
Seasons turned, life's relentless tide,
But fortunes dark, soon would collide.

His mother's demise, a hidden despair,
A sister's ill-fate, more than he could bear.
His brother adrift, in life's unfair snare,
His father's passing, a burden rare.

Rejected by love, for tradition's cruel bind,
Yet, undeterred, love still filled his mind.
Through seasons' change, he remained kind,
In love's labyrinth, his path wind.

Life's canvas changed, yet the sea stood still,
Friends wed, in life's unyielding drill.
Comrades lost to matrimonial thrill,
His heart, once full, now a silent shrill.

Children matured, elders left the stage,
His annual visits, now a forgotten page.
Alone on the beach, a heart caged in rage,
His tears unseen, in life's backstage.

His final leave, a month of grey,
His silent departure, nothing to say.
Regret lingers, for my unspoken goodbye that
day,
A guilt that in my heart will forever stay.

Back at camp, a final blow to his soul,
Abandoned by all, in life's relentless toll.
A heart shattered, beyond any console,

At twenty-nine, death took its toll.

A casket arrived, with memories so few,
His life's possessions, nothing new.
Dismissed by many, treasured by the few,
An unsung hero, to his land true.

Decades have passed, no memorial stands,
In the annals of time, lost like sands.
Yet now we realize, with joined hands,
His legacy of love, in our hearts expands.

The Oracle Dance

The drums got faster and the music louder!
He danced with a 'kavadi'.

Tall on his shoulder, dipping
and swaying to the rhythm.

A spear pierced through one cheek to the other,
A lemon balanced on the sharp end of the metal.

He danced as if Lord Murugan himself was
within,
His long hair flying and swirling like a halo.

Clouds of dust rose around his spinning legs,
The temple's oil lamp light turned it all to gold.

People stopped their dance, stepping back,
Forming a circle of awe around him.

Decorated elephants nearby stood still,
The air filled with the scent of dust, ash divine!

People felt they were seeing a god in this man,
Praying, hands folded, some overwhelmed to
fainting!
Silence fell, but prayers filled the air,
Music and dance reached their peak.

As if the gods watched and were pleased,
They opened the heavens, blessing with brief
rain.

It lasted just a moment or two,
And as the rain fell, the oracle fell too!

Collapsing to his knees on the damp earth,
Still with the 'kavadi' on his shoulders!

Don't Complain, Be Grateful

Our Little Buddha is as serene as ever!
Even in this dark, bitter December dawn!??
"Can't complain, my dear", whispered the lord,
The first Noble Truth; "There's Suffering in
Life!"

"When the world around is ravaged by war,
When poor, hungry and homeless wander!
Warm in your bubble you call home!
How can you complain, my dear!"

"Frost and Chill are certain in Winter!
Suffering and Pain in Life and War!
Christmas is near, and New Year to cheer!
Don't Complain, Be Grateful my Dear!"

Under the mango tree

Lying on the sand beneath the vast sky,
I watched clouds form stories way up high.
Told that each shape held a secret to find,
I watched, hoping to uncover what lay behind
me.

Beneath the mango tree, fruits ripe and bold,
Pepper vines swayed in the heat untold.
Children played around in their own little space,
Throwing stones and sticks at the tree's embrace.

In our game of throws, everyone tried their best,
With strength and aim, we put it to the test.
Laughter filled the air, under the sun's warm
rays,

As mangoes tumbled down, in a sweet, juicy
race.

Juice stained our clothes, but we didn't mind,
Mango peels scattered around, a carefree kind.
Seeds flung far, with hopes they'd sprout,
Hidden fruits saved, with love, no doubt.

In this game beneath the mango's leafy dome,
We made memories, in our village summer
home.

Winter Dreams

In a house grand, with a library so wide,
A young girl found solace, with books by her
side.
Her introverted nature, in solitude found peace,
In the world of words, her loneliness did cease.

She loved the winter, and poetry's gentle call,
As snow draped everything, in a silent, white
shawl.
Mountains, grass, and roads, all under snowy
layers,
The world outside her window, a scene of quiet
prayers.

As the sky and earth merged in a white embrace,
She watched, wrapped in warmth, in her cozy
place.

Bare branches held snowflakes, in a delicate hold,
A dance of nature, quiet, serene, and bold.

The wind whispered softly, snow tumbling from the trees,
Branches clapped gently, in the winter's breeze.
In this quiet world, under blankets snug and tight,
She found her joy, in the winter's silent kiss.

Formless Twins

I saw a thought one day, clear and bright,
A new idea, separate from my usual sight.
Around me, thoughts gathered, then faded away,
Leaving me with a sense of new thoughts at
play.

I penned a theory, neither original nor profound,
In my notebook, where my insights were bound.
'Soul and thoughts are the formless twins
Both are looking for bodies!'

Thoughts need expression, like the soul in flesh,
Through words spoken, written, a mesh.
Unrecorded, some thoughts wither and die,
While others in books, forever live.

Lost are countless thoughts, through time's
sieve,
Languages and beliefs that no longer live.
Thoughts, like spirits, roam, seeking minds to
fill,
Good ones wait, bad ones intrude at will.

Divine thoughts need an invite, a prepared mind,
Only then can their unique expression find.

Years later, I mused on thought's flow,
Like a radio tuned right, for ideas to grow.

Unacted, unnoticed, thoughts can fade,
Starting again their desperate parade.
Recorded thoughts, a treasure hidden deep,
In words and songs, their magic we keep.

I wondered, how to grasp this vast expanse,
Of thoughts uninvited, given no chance.
My brain, a vessel of undigested notions,
Overflowing with uncontrolled emotions!

Eyes of Soul

My childhood village isn't the same,
Years have passed, and it's changed since!
Gone for long, I come back to find,
Old memories are now hard to rewind.

In this place, filled with past tales,
Lives a friend, whom darkness veils.
Blind since teen, in a world unseen,
Yet, in our hearts, memories have been.

Through the eyes of the soul, we see,
A village, timeless, as it used to be.
If he could see, in this changed place,
Would he feel lost, out of trace?

Wishing to see through his soul's view,
Rebuild our past, in morning dew,
To spend a day in that old space as a child
with friends unchanged in frozen time's
embrace.

My Guru

They questioned him,
One long passed away.
They still ask him,
He who remains among us.
Many queries float by,
Unperturbed by answers or doubts.

Yet, some linger,
Some truly matter:
Is it Monotheism, or Polytheism?
Perhaps both, and Atheism too!
Form or the Formless?
Both exist in harmony.

Vishnu, Shiva, or Kali?
They are all parts of the same.

Man or God?
Human, Divine, and Avatar alike.
Krishna, Allah, or Christ?
All are facets of one truth.

Here or the Hereafter?
This life and beyond.
Black or White?
Every shade in between.
My faith or Yours?
Ours, theirs, everyone's!

Eastern or Western?
Local and global wisdom.
Man or Woman?
All ages, all genders.
Love or Renunciation?
Both paths lead to the divine.

Action or Devotion?
Engagement, prayer, and insight.
Dvaita or Advaita?
Dual, non-dual, and qualified non-dual.
Knowledge or Experience?
Both guide us on our path.

My truth or Your truth?
Individual and collective realities.
Idol worship or not?

Form and the Formless!
Is this Maya or Real?
Illusion and reality, intertwined.

"Have you seen God?"
Yes, he has.
"Is God real?"
Undoubtedly.
"How real?"
More real than our very existence.

I bow to thee, Guru,
Sri Ramakrishna Paramahansa

The Revolutionary Monk

In lands chained under a dark cloud of tyranny,
A humble beacon rose, strong and free.
Not born of royalty or halls of learning,
But a young monk, with a destiny burning.

From British India, his quest unfurled,
Touching hearts in America and Britain.
Armed not with a sword but with intellect's
might,
His tools were passion and resolve, shining
bright.

Wise beyond years and a sagely in name,
With a scientist's spirit, winning intellectual
acclaim.

With the heart of a warrior, brave and royal,
He lit the fire of hope, to oppressors disloyal.

Wandering lands, in years quickly passed,
He planted patriotism's seeds, hopes amassed.
His voice, a clarion call, far and widespread,
Igniting a nation's pride, long thought dead.

From his call, thousands rose, inspired,
One among them, with zeal never tired.
No armies, no war cries in the air,
Yet an empire bowed, to people's hearts!

In this monk's heart, a revolution took flight,
From his steadfast spirit, a nation's plight turned
bright.
A monk, a revolutionary, in history's adorned
hall,
A nation was reborn, answering his call.

A Chariot's Odyssey

In ancient India's mystical forests.
A story was told, revealing truths sublime.
Yama, the grave God of Death, and young
Nachiketa, old sage's wise and fearless son!

Wisdom from the Katha Upanishad unfolds,
In Sankhya philosophy, where mystery holds.
The story of a chariot and a sacred quest!
Sheds light on life and its meaning at its best.

See the chariot, our body's symbol,
drawn by five horses, sense organs!
Eyes, nose, tongue, ears, and skin,
Leading us astray again and again!

The reins, our mind, in control's embrace,
with intellect, the driver, setting the pace.
The soul, a quiet traveller seeking the true,
Aiming for the Supreme, in view!

In life's path, both good and pleasant lie,
The thoughtful mind discerns as time goes by.
The wise seek good, leaving pleasant aside,
While dull souls choose ease, letting true good slide.

This chariot's tale reveals life's deep secret,
Shows a way to rise above and not to fret.
Mastered senses, clear mind and intellect
finds the path to joy, leaving illusions behind!

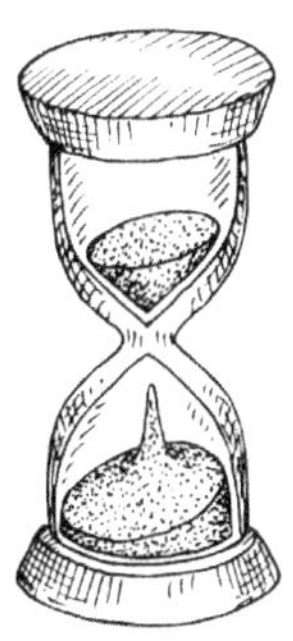

A Divine Query

Once upon a time, in an exotic land at a sacred moment,
Divine posed the devout a query, soft as a blessing!

"What are we, you and I, in this cosmic dance?
Reveal your heart and your head, dear devotee."

Bowed devotee "I am a servant to You, I humbly bow,
Sometimes, am a fragment of Your infinite expanse.

Yet, at times...forgive my ignorance, Lord, when
lost in a mystical trance...You and I are One!
Yes, One, my Lord!!"

"Which bond of the three, dear one, do you hold
dear?"
"The first one," he whispered, "Why dear?"
queried Lord!

Because I found in servitude, pride finds no
room,
And always in humility, I feel Your grace."
"Speak more," urged the Divine in a tender tone,
"Unveil the depths of wisdom you've known."

"In deeds and prayers, I think I am None,
but a servant to Your will, night and day!

In the stillness when meditation embraces,
I realise I am a soul, a part of Your grace.

Yet, swimming in Samadhi's profound sea,
I know I am Atman, and You and I are One!

In a Divine smile, the veil of Maya dropped
Advaita, Devotee and Divine became One!

One Last Goodbye

The wind paused, still and silent,
Night creatures listened, a hushed audience.
On the balcony, I sat, waiting,
Eyes fixed on the funeral site below.

Past midnight, the village and house, deep in
sleep,
I awaited a moment, a presence, a sign,
The moon ascended, casting a soft glow,
But he did not come!

Coconut leaves shimmered under moonlight,
Night-blooming flowers opened their eyes.
A week prior, my father waited late into the
night,
Ensuring I was home before locking the gate.

When I departed for work abroad,
I touched his feet, shared a final embrace,
Unaware it was our last goodbye.
Now, here I sat, waiting again.

Once fearful of the dark,
Now alone in moonlit shadows,

Longing for a sign, a spirit, a farewell.
Calm yet uncertain, I pondered.

Was that a chill I felt around me?
The wind's embrace or something more?
Why did slumber take me then?
Trees whispered secrets, night creatures
murmured.

The air filled with an unfamiliar fragrance,
Night flowers exuding their nocturnal perfume.
A hush fell, enveloping the night,
As the moon withdrew behind a cloud!